MW01230146

This Galaxy of Shards

Spiritual Poems by

Cherie Konyha Greene

Copyright © 2024 Cherie Konyha Greene All rights reserved

"Epiphany, Partly Cloudy" *The Christian Century*, January 1999. Print. Used by permission.

No part of this book may be reproduced, or stored in a retrieval system, or transmitted in any form or by any means, electronic, mechanical, photocopying, recording, or otherwise, without express written permission of the publisher.

ISBN-9798346690177

Printed in the United States of America

Contents

Dust

Remember that you are dust,
Made of the same atoms
As these ashes, as
A spoon, a bar of chocolate, a spider,
Your dog. You are
An amalgamation of particles,
Particulate matter,
Grains and motes of matter
Not to be swept
Under a rug, not
Into a dustbin, but
molded
Into strangely sentient form.
You are not without form,
Nor are you void
Because one day God
Looked upon Their
Arrangements of atoms and saw
A lack of you. And God said,
Let there be you.
And there was you.
It is no mean thing
To be dust.
Indeed, dust
Is everything.

Capernaum

"There was in their synagogue a man with an unclean spirit, and he cried out..."

We don't call them demons anymore,
When you're raving, howling out your reality
To the pious void. In our less benighted time,
This is not an unclean spirit but a case
Of schizophrenia, a distressing medical phenomenon,
Treatable with the new
Alchemy of neurotransmitters. You don't
Need an exorcism. Take your meds.
Be silent and come out. And yet,
There is some verity that will not be quieted, even
With Lithium. The words
Of the rebuked disorder are
Recorded for the ears of generations.
While those in their right minds,
Impressed by the magic trick,
Miss the unplumbed secret, that this
Weirdo from Nazareth
Has, in fact, come to scour out uncleanness
Of every kind. These supposedly sane folks
Make Jesus a star,
Yet they don't perceive the convulsive radiance shaking
The poor madman, who knows
Holiness when he sees it, perhaps because he walks closer
To the edge of darkness than others, closer
To where the light
Smashes its way in, slashing the cushions
And tossing the drawers
Of an untidy soul, leaving a salutary
Silence of truth in its wake.

Windfalls

Maybe you and a couch-
Surfing roommate are eking out
A hand to mouth garret
Subsistence like a bad song from
Rent in a tiny, badly painted
One-bedroom storefront,
With a disenameled clawfoot tub
Where the water never quite steams,
Over the barber shop, where
The stylist tells you cold water
Is good for your hair, but you know
It's because the shared water heater
Is defective, and all your hard-earned
Macaroni was just yesterday destroyed
By infant cockroaches, and
Your dancing goldfish Polycarp can't
Dive anymore, and your old miniature
Upright is still out of tune
When you play from the tattered 1940 hymnal, and
You're out of quarters for laundry, so
Wet socks are hung from the
Lampshades—today you find yourself
Under the neglected apple tree
In the park two doors down,
Where many ripe fruits have fallen, bruised and
Deformed, but true enough apples, and your
Eye-on-the-sparrow faith burgeons
At these priceless windfall gifts
From the Entwives, and you hunter-gather
Them shamelessly in a ragged
Shopping bag, take them home,
Slice them and cook them. You can live
For up to three days
On applesauce and optimism.

11

Prayers for Marco Polo

A picture I took a dozen years ago
And saved as my desktop background:
Five Tibetan prayer flags, strung across the flower boxes
Of two Turkish windows
In the narrow alley of an Italian city,
Primary colors frozen in mid-flap,
Spreading strength and compassion
On the saline wind of a Venice afternoon.
Bromeliads, succulents, palms and shamrocks
Share the terracotta planters in
Cosmopolitan camaraderie.
Most of the stucco is gone from the lower bricks,
Victim of the highest tides and of the long tearing of time.
A vestigial clothesline dangles from an iron ring.
And while I paused there with camera shutter opened,
I almost forgot that Somebody lives there.
Now, for all these years, I've wondered about
Whoever dwells behind those windows,
This grower of international greenery,
A Venetian Buddhist perhaps, an heir to Marco Polo
The bringer of the East to the West,
A child of the world surely, broadcasting
Peace and goodwill over the ancient floating stones.
I find myself drowning in envy
That they are able to open those windows and breathe
The sea-salt air I crave. Why
Has it not occurred to me before
To pray for this kind Anonymous
Who has been brightening my work days
With their unabashedly reverent colors?
Should I not be thanking the good Lord
For this captured moment of I and Thou,
For this merry faith-bridge of sighs
Too deep for words?

Rose

It surfaced unbidden
One warm, late vernal day, among
The blonde-bearded irises,
Just behind the frothy
Azaleas, a thorny growth, unplanted
By human hands,
Bearing one dainty, perfect magenta
Rosebud. In due time,
Called upon by the buttery sun,
The bud unfurled its tiny,
Flawless flags among the daylilies
and shamelessly showed
The secret golden stamens,
The furred depths that the hybrid teas hide
Under their modest drapery.
A simple, meticulous rose, heraldic, essential
In itself, an ur-rose, an early climber,
Alone that summer, but holding
Fragrant promise for coming Junes.
A weed, perhaps, to some, but
Spared and watered,
Tied to an encouraging frame,
It rewarded my forbearance
With a spontaneous firework of fuchsia
the next year. Now,
Three more Summers along, my voluntary rose
Has overgrown its iron trellis and needs
Some pruning, as its far-stretching thorns
Are a hazard to the good neighbors,
The ones with tidy beds of
Palliative pansies, the ones who
Mow and trim and weed, who
Would probably have pulled up my rose
With its invasive prickles and its
Lone, paltry bud

As an undisciplined interloper.
But it is the pride of my garden now,
Durable and intrepid and showy,
Brazen in its brave, wine-toned riot,
And I wouldn't swap it for all the careful
Cultivars in the White House,
My perfect gift from the good
Lord of perfection,
My ambassador from Pan, my
Sweet, sweet half-wild rose.

Bread

Sometimes
When I'm huddled
Under my solitary broom tree of despair,
It takes a great effort to look up
From the hot, yellow dust, to open
My fatigue-caked eyes and notice
The bread of life baked
On the hot stones of endurance,
And still more effort
To take a bite, even knowing
That this is Waybread, and a little
Can take me far, and that they
Who eat of it will never hunger,
Sometimes
Even with the living water
Cold in the sweating jug
And the cakes sweet and warm and new,
Eating seems a hard task.
Insurmountable.
I know about the journey ahead,
And an adventure looks like nothing
But a tired aching, a wearing down
Of joint and will.
Sometimes
Not even the voice of God will stir me to
Rise up and see the ready sustenance.
But then, at last, I catch a whiff
Of the glorious, fragrant and enlarging yeast,
And I manage to rouse my body for a nibble.
Only a nibble.
A few crumbs on my tongue,
A few cool drops,
And only then do I realize
That I am very hungry.

Ex Nihilo

Master, I know you are a hard man,
Reaping where you did not sow.

From bruised, windfallen apples grow fragrant trees;
From their dead and buried limbs are diamonds pressed.
From dish water flows fine wine,
From manure, rosebuds rise,
And from the atomic dustpan, spare stars are flung.

For you, the impossible springs effortlessly
From the formless and paltry.
The extravagant precisions
Of snowflakes, of galaxies, are a hobby
To while away eternity.
What could I add
From my one, cold, tarnished talent?

So here it is, Master.
I've kept it all safe for you.
Nothing got broken,
Not a drop was spilled.
Nothing wasted. Nothing lost.

But, then, Nothing was exactly what you started with.

A Dimly Burning Wick He Will Not Quench

I have seen the flame of your joy,
Steadfast as a menorah,
Hopeful as the first spark of vigil,
Fragile as a birthday wish,
And yet so bright.

For a lone tongue of fire,
Confidingly kindled,
Transforms darkness to Great Light.

I have seen your torch assailed,
Buffeted by tempests of trouble,
Snuffed under bushels of conformity,
Damped by downpours of tears,
And yet it burns.

I would be glass,
A translucent shield encircling,
Refracting this tender rushlight radiance,
Shielding and revealing.

For a clear lens,
Rightly rounded,
Transforms flicker to Pharos.

So let your light shine.

Temple Stones

"What large buildings!" They said
Just before the hurricane came through,
Before the wildfire raged,
"What large stones!"
Sinking beneath the rising ocean,
Falling from above!
The earth is in labor,
And it's only beginning.
With wars and rumors, and Jesus said
It will all come crashing down, all
Our temples and skyscrapers and grand
Gothic illusions.

Jesus and his hippie clown disciples
Once danced in a movie
Atop the twin towers, but now, as we know,
Not a rebar is left on a slab,
Not crashed down by weather but by
Human will.

By human will also
Comes the weather, a pouring flood
Of self-interest, a blowing vortex
Of avarice, we drill, baby, don't we,
Blasting and fracturing and pumping
To fill the maws of our impressively large
Machines? We wildly consume all before us, flames
Of our willful ignorance gobbling up
The birds of the air and the beasts
Of the field in the conflagration of our
Worldly cravings, blasting away
The rooftops of hope in the cyclone
Of our despair. We sell the world, consign it
To Hell for the price of an egg.

From such a birthing, what good thing
Can emerge? What rough beast
Will be Earth's next child?
Or can we provoke one another
To love and good deeds, can we
Cruise the open sea for olive branches,
Chart islands not of trash
But of compassion and grace and fresh water
As we see the Day approaching?

Christmas Eve Lectionary in Wartime

The people who walked in darkness
have seen a great light—
> A blast in the night,
> Fallen avenging angels
> In green-brown hordes
> Scalpel-stab the city while
> The cancer roams free—

For every boot of the tramping warrior in battle tumult,
And every garment rolled in blood—
> While the innocents scream
> No more, our cup has overflowed,
> The dying scholar at the crossroads
> Rolls to face the rattling guns
> Of a dying empire—

Will be burned as fuel for the fire.
For unto us a child is born—
> A lace-swaddled choirboy
> Guarded from Herod by wary guns
> Sings Ave Maria
> Mother of God, bear to us now
> The Prince of Peace.

Mustard

They say it's a weed,
An invasive shrub that
No one would plant on purpose.
The wild mustard seed
Dances on desert dust storms,
Lighter than a grain of clay,
Smaller than a period on a page
Of nine-point type.
It lands where the holy ghost wind wills,
And there it grows, bit
By bit into a tree with many
Birds' nests, shading the steaming,
Stinking sheep, the ravening goats,
The weary human,
Soon taking over the pasture,
Spreading its arms wide
As the wideness of Love Themselves,
Broad and high as the
Vastness of Mercy. All this
From a seed so small
You have to hold your breath
To look at one close up,
On the tip
Of a finger.
It starts
As a delicate thing, a thing
Of no consequence,
But this is divine deception,
For it surely grows.

BT's Lounge

It was only a block away from my flat,
Across Main Street and
Down the alley, underneath
A pan-Asian restaurant.
I don't remember the first time I went
On a Karaoke Saturday, only
That it became a religious observance.
Singing Karaoke Saturday night,
Singing in Choir Sunday morning.
The place was not much to look at.
Dim, to hide the stains on the painted concrete floor,
A stumpy, u-shaped bar and a scattering
Of mismatched chairs at
Sticky formica tables.
A pool table missing a few solid balls
And one striped.
If you were very brave or very hungry,
You could order sushi or
Crab rangoon from upstairs.
In one corner,
There was a red vinyl half booth
Salvaged from some dead diner, where
A generously curvy young woman
Worked the enchanted song machine.
And all the regulars sang, some
The same song week after week, some not,
I sang a different song each time.
When Robin Williams died, I sang Tears of a Clown.
Most of us took our karaoke careers
Very seriously, and some of us were
Also good. Many were horrendous.
Their assault on Apollo should have gotten them arrested.
As might the flagrant sex
Happening in the parking lot
Between the red pickup trucks.

I once got hit on by a gentleman
Who claimed
With a straight face
That his name was Christian Grey.
I told him
This was not alluring to an English major
With a writing MFA.
He didn't understand what I said.
I found a new wobbly bar stool.
You see, all the capital city misfits were there,
The shy, curly-haired girl, the
Cuba Gooding Jr. lookalike,
The trans lady still going by a boy's name,
Not yet certain who she was, the
Angry misogynist lad,
The middle-aged recent divorcee (me), all
Serenading one another with rap and rockabilly and
Leonard Cohen, writhing
Like drunken bellydance dervishes,
And it was a grubby little corner of Hell
When one disgruntled singer flung
Fat-phobic insults at the sweet DJ,
Their cruel beef spilling onto the sidewalk,
And it was also a very tiny
Fragment of sweat-stained Heaven when all these
Tender fallen angels
Were singing along
To Hallelujah.

The Third Sunday in Lent

I spied a spider on the altar cloth,
Eight crook-legs splayed like fault lines, loathsome, dark
Against the purple velvet sackcloth, mark
Of foulness on fair linen. I was loath
To let this smutty interloper stay
In holy precincts. Brush it off and tread
It underfoot! Protect the sacred bread!
But, wine being poured, I kept away.
The beast, drawn to its Source, ascended near
The Maker's blood, unconscious of defect.
The tiny publican showed less false fear
Than me, with penance lavishly correct,
So scrupulous against all things unclean.
My sacrilege of pride crept on, unseen.

Maundy

It's not meant to be comfortable
Or comforting. Feet are stinky
And hairy.
They hold lint.
They grow fungi.
They step in things they shouldn't,
Like mud and cat barf.
Washing them should be awkward.
It should make your skin crawl a little.
Getting them washed should be
Profoundly embarrassing.
You should be as flipped out as
Peter was with his dusty sandals off and
Jesus reaching down his holy hands,
Towel at the ready,
To scrub the camel dung
From Peter's toenails.
But that's what he commanded us to do:
Pollute your hands, cloud the water
With sweat and debris.
Rinse, repeat,
Over and over, for as many feet
As you can find,
Until all soles everywhere
Shine with newborn newness,
Because the master who first
Washed yours is
Bathing them still, forever
Drowning them, shrouding them,
And bidding them rise.

Triduum

"He Took a Towel"

The floor's as cold as penance
To feet just out of winter
From the swaddling of wool socks
And snow boots, the toes
See that they are naked,
And are afraid.

The towel is so white.

Stripping the Altar

Before the horror of your loss, we flee.
Take cover! In the basement there's a shelter.
The holy ark is rifled!
Evacuate the chalice!
Candles, linen, cushions, pulpit, books,
They all retreat from Passion's deadly blast.

I fetch the vinegar and soak the sponge
To scour away the scandal of your pain,
        This little light of mine,
        I let them blow it out,
Gone into hiding under blackout rules.
My God, my God, we have forsaken you.

And all is cold, hard pavement bricks and stone
Outside the High Priest's palace, where we cringe
        Beside the dull coals, trembling,
        With eyes fixed on the wet floor,
And ears deaf to the rooster's hue and cry,
Hoping Death will pass over once more.

Venerating the Cross

Affectionate splinters
Cold and sharp on my lips
A moment of shrinking
Into blackness, tripping
Over this sudden and ludicrous love,
And I fall to the bricks.

(Sometimes it causeth me to tremble.)

Then the line moves on.

Stations

Pursuing a large log cross down the busy,
Pot-holed street, sirens passing,
(Rushing off to some new Passion
We may never read of in the Union Leader),
Marking the dumpy bus stops on the road
To the place of the skull,
Knee-sore and hip-weary, doggedly
Trailing behind our fellow flagellants,
We pray.

Such desperate prayers.
Dear God, change our world.
Fix us so we can change it.
We stop, in turn, at schools and
Parks and Projects, beseeching God
To infuse us with the changing force
Of his own suffering,
Which certainly trumps anything
My limbs and lungs endure here,
Begging to be the hands of change.

Passersby, when they don't
Turn their heads and pass by
On the other side,
Offer accusing looks.
"Nice cross," I expect they're thinking.
"Nice litany. Nice bishop. And now
What? What have your prayers
To do with us? Our school
Is about to close, our only food store is
Boarded up, and our parkland is
Full of freezing tents. Fix those things
With your prayers."

And we hear your glares

Loud and clear. We also feel
Powerless. Prayer
Seems our sole weapon
Against the creeping darkness
That's trying to consume you.
We know we are bystanders
To Christ's passion, and bystanders
To that of our own neighbors.
We think if we follow and weep
We're doing something helpful.
But please, don't sneer, show us
How we can pull you down from
Your crosses, or at least
Like Veronica
Wipe your blood-trailed faces.

Look, I brought a handkerchief.
(It was for my nose.)
I brought a staff.
(It was for my legs.)
I brought water
(for my lips.)
Are you thirsty?

On the Third Day

Out of the vacuum of light, into the black ice cave,
Within one stone cold Body:
      A flame!

From the ignited center
      The Blood!

      (As snow in a warm hand pools, acquires motion,
           Accelerates through fingers and sleeves)

      The Blood

Begins to flow. In dim awareness, he is reassembled.
      There are my Arms!
              My Knees!
      My Nose!

      This   is   my   Body.

Nerves recharging, he tries
      A Finger!
      A Foot!
      An Elbow!

Once more straining limbs against space, he stands.
Outside in the gray morning garden, the Stone

(which had begun rapidly to grow moss)

Rolls.

      Over.

And in the doorway appears

A Man!

Who slips quietly down to the road where
       (if you stood long enough
        In the place where he had stepped)

You might see the early thaw grow

      Lilies!

Through the ancient Pavement.

Whom   do you seek   in the tomb?

Easter Daffodils

At the Morton Arboretum, Lisle, Illinois

Green-skirted ladies gavotte in a gust
Of the brazen wind of Spring begun.
Gloria trumpets rise up from the dust
Like wide-strewn particles of the sun,
Conserving its glow when a fresh wind turns
And the dark grumbles down with steely cold.
Their golden fire in the cloud's face burns,
Defying hard-headed winter's hold.
The dark is fresh and full of threat.
Spring's promise is in the hope of doom,
That something will be different yet,
And dance out again from the garden tomb.

The Relics of St. Mark

I got my sneakers wet in Venice.
Outside the bridal cake Basilica,
Fresco-frosted, sprinkled with spoils,
Trying to understand about relics.
To imagine people
So swooningly
Enamored of God
They would do absolutely
Anything
To be near what They had touched.

Yes! The hucksters would annunciate,
He really did become flesh and dwell among us.
His Mother lactated; here's her milk!
He really was crucified and died
On solid wood from a solid tree; here's a splinter!
On the third day, he really rose again,
Emerging to life from the burial cocoon;
Here's his face on the shroud!

And he had friends, among them
One who flew
From the garden, naked, leaving his clothes in the grasp
Of the astonished centurion;

One who flew
From trouble with the Apostle
(Being scolded for a cowardly lion), who flew
On, until he understood that the wings he was flying on
Were God's,
And then the Apostle, now in trouble, called to him
To fly to his aid.

(And maybe, who knows,
Along the way grounded here in the mud,

Complaining that he'd be stuck forever
In this treacherous bog, maybe, who knows,
Someone taking the complaint as prophecy.)

One who roared out
The scandal of mercy, the terror of resurrection,
The alarming words of God made flesh, who flew
A last flight into Egypt, to roar some more before dying,
Wings folded away,
Somewhere between Pharos and desert. Yet,
As often happens with God's friends,
The roar still echoed
Over the sea to these snug, soggy streets, and
Into the ears of traders who coveted those wings.

So then flying once more, not by choice, embarked
On one more ship, dead flesh disguised by dead flesh,
Slipped out by stealth, leaving his shroud in the grasp
Of the astonished invader. Well, why not, then?
Fly from their mainmast, get them back to that
Impossible island of theirs.

He'd known he'd end up in that mud someday.

So I paid my indulgence of Euros and stopped for a visit.

In all that gaudy confection of a place,
The one bit of plain, gray stone,
A tomb engraved with the plea of the Apostle
Who had once sent him packing,
"Mark, come help me."

Outside, the same sea that had borne these relics
Out of Egypt
Was creeping under the door of the lady chapel.
I stepped out into the flood,
Where the air was filled with flying

Lions, and felt all of it:
Garden, terror, scolding, words, mud, shroud,
Meat, mast, corpse, wings, roars
Fill my shoes in a world where holiness
Is as tangible, intrusive and chilling
As wet sneakers.

God Is Knocking On My Head

If I let you in, what will you do?

Will you scrub like an angry hurricane,
Sweep out the fairy dust,
Nail down loose assumptions, and
Draw masking conclusions
Over the windows? Or

Will you rage like twin kittens,
Upset the salt-of-the-earth shaker,
Tip my ass over your teakettle, and
Knock my Ming sanity
Off the lampstand? Or

Will you creep,
(please) stalk,
And catch my conscience
Unready (shutters open), and

Blow

A kiss?

Devil

Last night I dreamed
Or didn't dream
That the front door was left open,
And I woke, or didn't wake,
And rose to shiver in the drafty living room.
I reached past the recliner to push it shut, and saw there,
Clinging to the upper screen with its claws,
A murky form, blacker than the sky behind it.
Too big for a cat.
Too fat and too dark.
Malice seemed to ooze from its
Unseen mouth, to creep like smoke
Around its likely fangs. I recalled
A piece of Caribbean cultural appropriation
I learned in a church choir--
>   *Shut the door,*
>   *Keep out the devil.*
As one digited paw slid toward the crack,
As the creature shifted its weight,
I pushed with all my little might
To slam the door hard,
Twist the knob lock and
Wish this door had a dead bolt.
To find my breath. Later,
When the sky turns gray and pale, and
The phone alarm plays Benny Goodman,
I click on the lamp and dismiss the phantom as a skunk.
A skunk with a 5 foot jump?
And no stripe?
Or a fisher cat maybe, leaping at doors
For no reason? I mean,
How could anything seriously evil be present
In the same house with "Sing, Sing, Sing,"
The happiest piece of music ever written?
But I can still smell

Something.
Skunk, then.
Has to be.
To freshen the room
I burn a cone of nag champa,
Match shaking in lamplight.
The West Side Devil, I'll call it, this heavy
Darkness pleading at my door,
Grasping, waiting, reaching...

> *Shut the door.*
> *Keep out the devil.*
> *Shut the door,*
> *Keep the devil in the night,*
> *Shut the door,*
> *Keep out the devil.*
> *Light the candle,*
> *Everything's all right*
> *Light the candle,*
> *Everything's all right*

Epiphany–Partly Cloudy

The people who walk in darkness
        Are coiling up their strings
        Of deluxe miniature cool-burning
        Lights,
        And looking for the sun
        To return by Eastern Airlines
        From his Florida Solstice.

At four o'clock, blinds down and lamps lit,
I'm folding gold foil paper,
        Wrapping the crèche in swaddling tissues
        And vacuuming up dead needles
        From the tree of life.
Behind the hum of Hoover
I overhear my throat
        Still singing
        Veni, veni . . . (as if he never had)
Like most productive citizens of Bethlehem,
(those not watching their flocks by night)
I was baking fruit and nut bread,
        Filling out paperwork for Caesar,
        Sending formal greetings to distant relations,
        Navigating the marketplace for the best price
On frankincense,
When the Gloria
Passed through town.

Following stars is something you can do
When you live in a desert.

Enfolded in Great Lakes fog, I follow
        The taillights of the Ford ahead of me
        Until the church's white gravel drive
        Creeps out of the haze and climbs its hill.
Inside the sanctuary are spotlights and candles,

And I am informed, and inform you,
With all due pageant, song and reverence,
That Unto Us a Child is Born.
Then home for turkey
À la king
And off to Marshall Field's
To return Aunt Mary's myrrh.

From a well-salted parking lot
In a land without sun,
Outside the lower entrance of Sears and Roebuck,
I lower my parka hood
And tilt my head back,
Looking for a star.

The Ballad of Steve T.

Can't you hear that whistle whine,
Sounding like the steel is crying
For the melancholy deed it will perform,
As his blood slickens the track
And the driver pulls the brake
Of the train that would take one gay Christian home?

Church ladies all around me,
Printing pulp theology
Under contract to the straight and narrow way,
Heard the locomotive scream,
And the old one said, "I dreamed
Some poor college boy was gonna die today."

     Then profs were weeping in the chapel
     How poor Stevie's in the morgue,
     While Trustees went on the record:
     It's a sin against the Lord;
     He won't let them in the Kingdom,
     We don't let them in the dorms.
     After all, if they'd just pray, they could reform.

They say he knelt as if to pray
As the engine rolled his way,
With his arms for blessing crossed upon his breast.
Sweet Lord, forgive this sin,
Because he knew he'd never win.
His options were to die or to transgress.

That was twenty years ago,
And we think we're better now,
We've all learned the bitter lesson of the lost.
They've got a bishop in New Hampshire.
See? We've learned to love our neighbor.
Then we find another young one on the cross.

And they're weeping in the chapels
Over students under palls,
And the old men make pronouncements
In the classrooms and the halls.
People say you must be perfect.
People say you must conform.
While the Father's rushing arms cry,
      "You are home."

Butterflies

I know a man who dislikes butterflies.
He says he doesn't trust their brilliant hues,
Their tiger stripes and tails and cobalt blues.
He says their glorious splendor is all lies,
A nasty prank they play on our dull eyes
So we forget the disconcerting clues,
Like their legs and faces, that their true
Nature is insectoid. With wings they rise
Above their station, these bedazzled bugs
Who not so long ago were merely worms,
Creeping down leaves and munching on green things.
Beauty? My friend declared, those ugly mugs
Can't be disguised. I said, but this world turns
On transformation, here where worms grow wings.

Transfiguration

I noticed this year
That the feast of the Transfiguration
Falls during Carnival time,
The time of masks that reveal.
Jesus goes up a hill with three
Sleepy friends
And wakes them up with the sparkle of his
Glowing glory costume.
Masked in light,
He shows his reality,
And groggy Peter,
Seeing the apparent masquerade of
The heroes of his faith
Along with his own rabbi,
Thinks that of course they should make booths,
(Confusing Purim with Sukkot?)
Anything to make this
In-
credible sight
Fit into his bleary universe.

But the universe is what is clear,
It is human sight
That is bleary,
Groggy and quotidian,
Truth is in the assumed glory
The mask of lightness and
Kinship and
Pronounced favor

Carnival of Nicaea

I believe in one God,
The Begetter, the all-potent,
Whose ecstasy big-
Banged heaven and earth,
All that is, masked and naked, material and mythic.

I believe in one Lord of Misrule, Jesus (H) Christ,
The only off-Spring of the fountain-Head,
Perpetually propagated from the Progenitor,
Seed from seed, sunbeam from sunbeam,
True Love from true Love,
Ejaculated, not manufactured,
Of one organism with the Origin.
Through him all bits and pieces were assembled.

For us and for our regeneration
He tumbled down from cloud nine.
By the potency of the holy poltergeist,
He made a meat mask from the damsel Maria
And was made a Fool.
For our felicity he was clobbered and strung up
By Punch-us Pilate;
He bit the dust and was shrouded and planted.
On the count of three he burst out
In accordance with the script.
He leapt, bounced and rocketed into Bliss
And is positioned at the right flank of Ardor.
He will emerge again in brilliance to audition
The lively and the lifeless,
And his free greased Tuesday will come to no conclusion.

I believe in the divine fire Joker, the Head,
The donor of animation,
Who springs from the Sire and the Spawn.
With the Sower and the Seed he is venerated and fêted.

He has ventriloquized the oracles.

I believe in one dedicated dappled and
Disseminated krewe.
I embrace one drenching for the deletion of depravity.
I look for the arousal of the rags and bones,
And the animation of the Comedy to come.

Amen.

Saints 1

For all the brave saints who
Break the rules of hate,
Loving hazardously, dying
To selves for the sake of your intrepid Name,
Your Name be praised.

For all the simple saints who
Forsake near pleasure, rising
To embrace unclean people and
Feeding lions for the sake of your fierce Name,
Your Name be praised.

For all the sturdy saints who
Destroy small deaths, growing
As trees by the water, then
Being felled for the sake of your stout Name,
Your Name be praised.

For all the tender saints who
Fall beneath the harsh law, throwing
Their soft selves on the hard road,
Being trodden for the sake of your gentle Name,
Your Name be praised.

For all the unsound saints who
Stiffen their Pharisee necks, aiming
To impose human order on the Chaotic Good
For a mistaken concept of your perfect Name,
Your Name still be praised.

Blessed are they who have much to learn, for
They shall know,
When they see you face to bare face,
The fierce joy of dying.

Blessed are they who are consumed, for
They shall know,
When you uphold their sacrificial hands,
The stout joy of providing.

Blessed are they who survive, for
They shall know,
When you gather their crowns at your unshod feet,
The intrepid joy of falling.

Blessed are they who don't survive, for
They shall know,
When you embrace their naked souls,
The gentle joy of rising.

Alleluia, alleluia.

Rock

At first I wasn't sure
What I was looking at
While my cold hand squeezed the cold
pump nozzle
And I wrinkled my nose at the fumes.
A thing on the grubby concrete platform
Brightly colored with
A red, white-dotted heart,
Various pink and white flowers,
Leaves, on a blue
Rock. Yes.
It was a rock.
A painted rock.
I suddenly recalled my sister
Commanding our father to stop the car
Outside the abandoned Baptist church in
Boyertown Pennsylvania,
Crying, "Rock! I see a rock!"
This was a Thing, apparently, in Boyertown,
To find and collect
And rehide painted rocks.
Could my gas station rock be
Related to those? (Yes,
I already thought of it as my rock,
Though clearly it was painted by someone else,
Someone who perhaps considered it theirs and
Had still left it
For me to happen upon.)
The rock felt
Good in my hand, solid,
Shapely,
I turned it over, saw a hashtag on a slip of paper
Beneath the shrink wrap.
So I put it in my car.
Drove it home.

Showed my roommates my prize.
They agreed
It was a very pretty rock,
Perhaps humoring me.
I got on Facebook and told the ether where
I had found it, posted a picture.
I kept telling myself I'd soon hide it again,
Pass along the joy of finding. But
Now it sits on my desk
Between the mouse and the tin of binder clips,
Watched over by a washcloth rabbit
Someone at the office made us all for Easter.
I hardly notice it half the time,
But I would miss it if
It weren't there.
It fills me with both delight
And guilt.
I feel a glutton for its beauty.
I keep saying
One of these days,
I'm going to hide it again
For some other lucky person to happen upon,
To be amused or bemused by, maybe
Make their whole day.
But what if it doesn't get found again?
What if no one else is
Observant enough?
What if it sits lonely on some brick wall or
Under some bush?
Do I have faith enough
In God or in my fellow humans
To let my rock go off on its own?

Clean

I

First, sulfur soap
To rid me of the red
Blemishes
That continue to appear anyway.
For the head, cool
Tea tree for my itchy
Color change hair—it
Hurts my eyes.
And for the rest of the skin,
Castile soap so pure
Hikers can clean their teeth with it.
I believe
All those labels, but
Once clean,
My flesh looks
Just the same.

II

Create in me a clean heart,
Scour away the tiny
White lies, the pomps
Of privilege, scrub
The righteous smugness off
My fragrant feet, and
Not my feet only, but also
My grasping hands and my
Proud head. Wash
Me, and I shall be clean in-
Deed,
And in word, for
To you all hearts
Are open.

III

First, create in me a clean
Sulfur soap heart, to rid me of
The tiny white blemishes,
The red lies
That continue to appear anyway,
Scour away the itchy color change pomps,
The cool tea tree privilege
That hurts my eyes.
Scrub the righteous smugness
Off my proud fragrant feet
My feet only but also
My grasping hands and my head,
And for the rest,
Wash me with soap so pure
Hikers' can clean their teeth. I believe
I shall be clean in-
Deed with it, and in word,
In all those labels, but
My flesh to you once clean,
All hearts open look
Just the same.

Holy Shit

Recently I heard someone ask
Whether God shits.
It was meant as humor, but
If you believe in the Incarnation
Then you know God did shit
As Jesus.

No one talks about that.
No one talks about Jesus' penis.
But of course he had one
By all accounts Jesus was a cis male,
Which is weird when you think
That God is beyond gender
And yet They chose to join the human race
As a baby boy

Or did They choose?
Maybe They gave random nature a chance,
Concentrating Their essence into
An undifferentiated embryo,
Waiting to see what would come shining
Out of poor Mary,
Unwed and pregnant in
A culture of honor killings.

Mary could have been stoned with God inside her
If Joseph weren't an uncommonly nice guy.

They needed to last
A few years on Earth
To get the humans to hear
Their lessons, and only then
Be crucified
And die bloody.

And so God was born bloody

In a cow trough,
Covered in the usual daily shit,
Human shit and bull shit,
God Themselves in a shitty diaper,
A distinct individual, Jesus,
Half in and half out of the "They" God also was, and
Already ready to die.

But not just yet.
There were things
He had to grow up and tell us, like
Don't take other people down,
Take yourself down a peg, you
Who think you're righteous.
(I'm paraphrasing here)
He said,
To be human
Is to take care of each other,
All the others,
Especially the Others.

He said,
If you want to be in charge,
Don't be.
The only power worth having
Is the power to love so hard
That you lose your grip
On what you think is life.

Then at last he gave up that grip to show us how.

And it's probable that, in giving up that ghost,
Considering the violence of the death,
The ruler of the universe
Pissed and shit Themselves.
Making piss and shit onto holy things.

Holy Shit.

Kaleidoscope

For Christine

What hand spins this
Galaxy of shards,

Smashed glass planets
Tumbling round the rough

Edges of this
Fractured sunlight and

Falling crystal
Leaves, turns us and shakes

And twists our bright,
Broken chaos down

Into perfect
Plane geometry,

Grinds translucent,
Mutable master-

Pieces from the
Jumble of sharp and

Colorful chance,
Changing from glory

Into glory
When the light breaks through?

Fusion

The eyes of lust burn sharper than the stars.
I lie with tremored limbs on this strange pyre,
Waiting for my comfortable scars
To be unformed and stripped of death desire.
Such stars are forged in fundamental fire
And blasted with a blaze so deadly hot,
A creature made of mud and meaty mire
Is turned to ashes, atoms, then to nought.
Much rarer is the miracle that's wrought
By rays of care that touch a clay-formed clod
Of nothing much and, like a dear thing bought,
Fire it to life. So burn the eyes of God,
Not to consume, but to kindle a sun
In kindly fusion, making split selves one.

Saints 2

For Wilma

By now you will have heard
Through the celestial grapevine
That I prayed for you after your homeward journey.
A papist heresy, yes.
Also an act of love.

We are so alike, you see, though also opposite.
We share the DNA of round bellies, of
Poor housekeeping, of
Steadfast affection.
I am your mother's granddaughter,
And I love you still.

When Saint Peter—sorry, Peter the Apostle—mentions that
He heard your name from the lectern of a church with a
Gay(!)
Bishop(!),

In the prayers for the departed(!),
You will know, now,
Know, down to your very genes
That I meant it when my friends prayed:

"For those who have died,
That they might have a place
In Your eternal kingdom."

See you there.
(!)

Made in the USA
Columbia, SC
20 November 2024

46609902R00033